MY F[...] A-Z

HIGH CONTRAST BABY BOOK

Ant

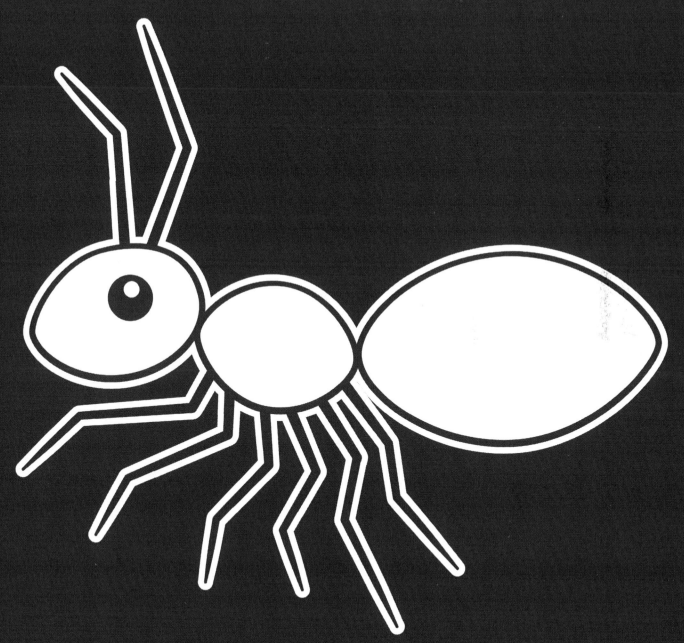

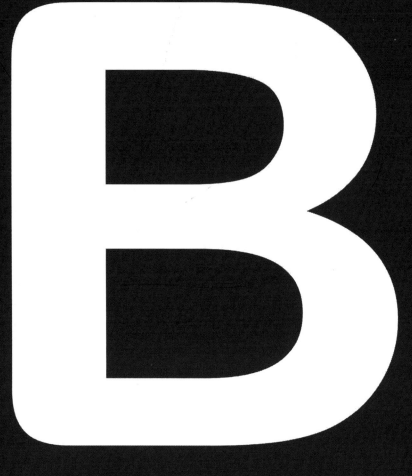

IS FOR

Ball

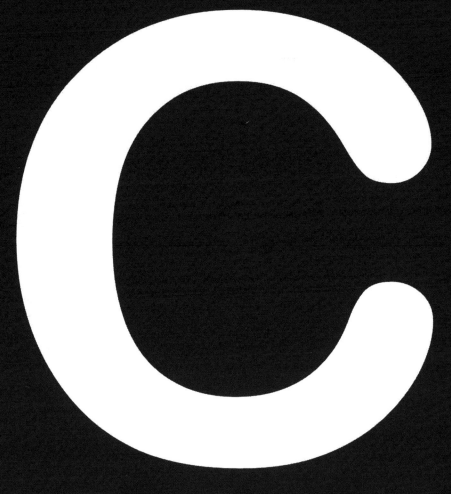

C

IS FOR

Cube

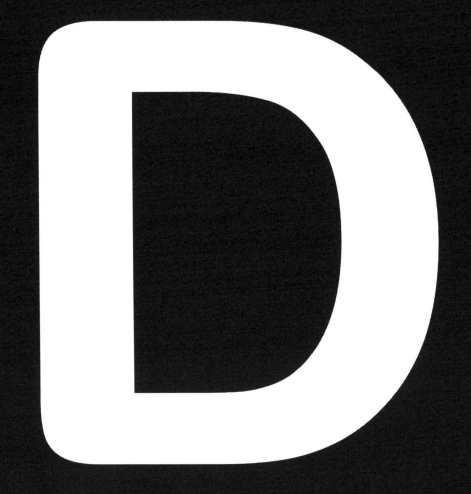

IS FOR

Dinosaur

IS FOR

Egg

IS FOR

Flower

G

IS FOR

Guitar

IS FOR

Heart

I

IS FOR

Ice cream

Ice cream

J
IS FOR

Jellyfish

Koala

L

IS FOR

Leaf

Mug

IS FOR

Nail

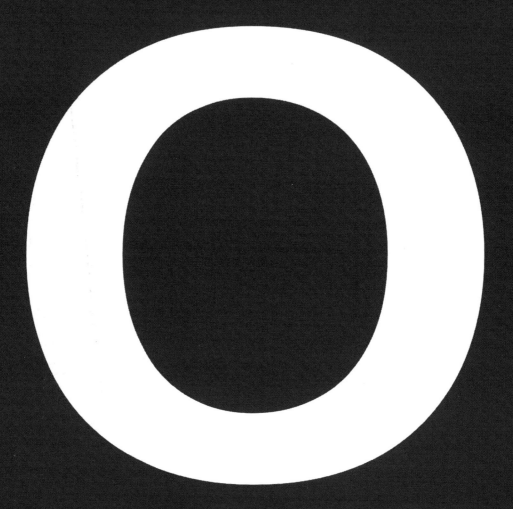

O

IS FOR

Octopus

P

IS FOR

Pear

IS FOR

Queen

R

IS FOR

Rocket

S

IS FOR

Star

IS FOR

Turtle

IS FOR

Umbrella

IS FOR

W

IS FOR

Watch

X IS FOR

X-ray

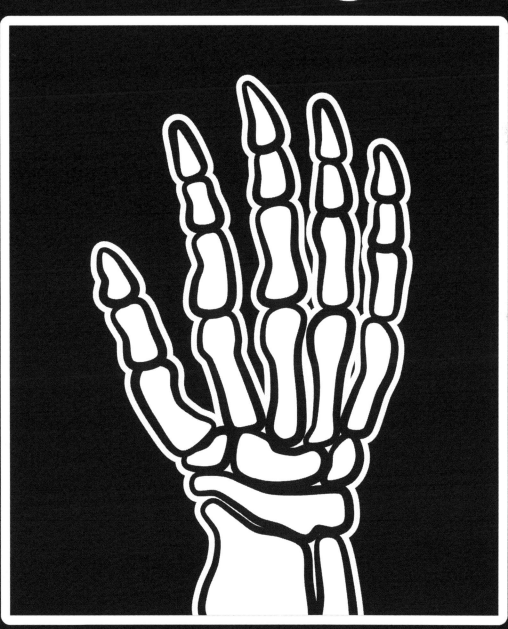

IS FOR

Yoyo

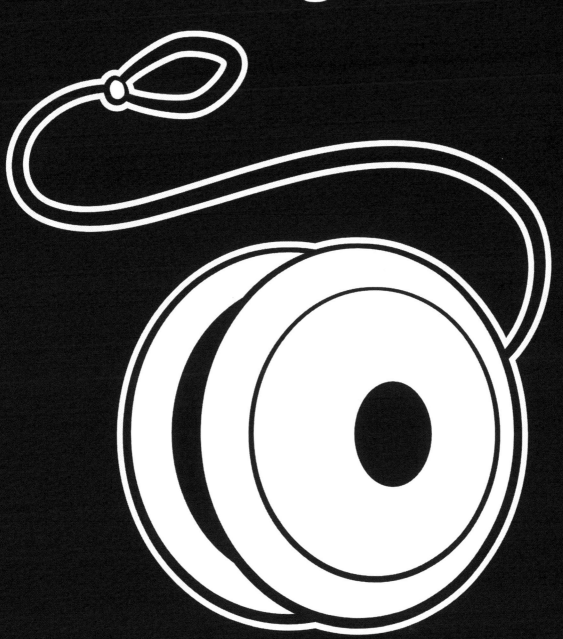

IS FOR

Zebra

If You are satisfied with the book, I will be grateful if You could take a moment to submit a review.

Manufactured by Amazon.ca
Bolton, ON

33570897R00031